BROKEN BUT FIXED

ENDORSEMENTS

Diane Dalton is a wonderful, solid Christian with great integrity and a hard work ethic. She has shown over many years of ministry that she is intent on being a positive example to other people of how to allow the Lord to use her to help other people navigate everyday needs and storms they face in life (especially those who are hurting, oppressed, homeless, and in need). She focuses on the Lord's plan for her life, pursues that calling through good times and bad, and accomplishes God's purposes in her life.

—**Randy and Karen Parlor**, MHC Neighborhood SENT Church Pastors

Diane is one of the kindest people I've met, and even though her journey has been difficult, she still chose to be a bright light for the most vulnerable. Diane is a perfect example of resilience and pure love.

—**Tamara Glenn**

Diane is a true inspiration to those who know her. As a mom of five children, she has taken on the challenge of raising a family while also making an incredible impact in her community. It is no surprise she was named "Greater Lansing Woman of the Year" for her leadership in "Into the Streets" and "House of Hope" where she has dramatically impacted those in need.

—**Judy Kehler**

BROKEN BUT FIXED

The Diane Dalton Story

DIANE DALTON

COPYRIGHT NOTICE

Cover and Interior Design: Derinda Babcock
Editor: Cristel Phelps

Library Cataloging Data
Names: Dalton, Diane (Diane Dalton)
Broken But Fixed / Diane Dalton
126 p. 23cm × 15cm (9in × 6 in.)
ISBN-13: 979-8-218-47151-4 (paperback) | 979-8-218-47152-1 (e-book)
Key Words: Growing up in an orphanage; childhood trauma; emotional abuse; restoration; memoir; wholeness; ministering to the broken

DEDICATION

I dedicate this book to my husband Paul, my best friend, and to our five children: Samara, Hezron, Eliza, Joseph, and Kathryn. I also thank God for our ten grandchildren who bring such wonderful joy into my life.

Contact: pdventures07@yahoo.com

ACKNOWLEDGMENTS

I want to thank Mount Hope Church and Pastors Dave and Mary Jo Williams, along with Pastors Kevin and Renee Berry for their vision and leadership in ministry. I would also like to thank Cristel Phelps, my favorite teacher from the Bible Training Institute, for all the teaching and classes that equipped me for the work of the ministry.

CHAPTER 1

AT THE BEGINNING

My story began in Chicago, Illinois, where I was born. I have two older sisters, Kathy and Sheila, and one brother, Don. Like so many others who have lived broken childhoods, time has passed, we have married, have families, and survived our childhood.

I am sharing my story with you to show you a little of what it was like to be a child growing up in an orphanage ... and the life God has given me beyond those years.

Our mother and father were very kind people who were hard working and considerate. My mom was a stenographer with the court system, and my father was a photo engraver. My aunts and uncles have always said they were the life of the party, amicable, with a great sense of humor.

We would go on family picnics. I remember one time they had a race going on in the park. All the five-year-old boys and girls were getting ready to line up. My dad said, "I know you're going to win, so I'll be at the finishing line waiting for you."

That was a special day for me. I did win the race and won a tea set. My daddy walked around with me and said, "Look at what my little girl won. She's such a strong and fast runner." These words meant so much to me in the years to come. When I became a track star, I always thought of how proud my dad would have been. Today, I feel my father is at that finish line still waiting for me.

My mother had a lovely personality. When she smiled, her face beamed, showing how happy she was to be a mother, wife, and homemaker. They were both very loving and kind parents. I thank God for those memories because things were about to change.

DIANE'S PARENTS' WEDDING PICTURE

CHAPTER 2

MOTHER'S CONDITION

My mom was diagnosed with breast cancer when I was six-years-old. My main memories of her were her travels back and forth to the Billings Hospital in Chicago. When she came home, I was her little nurse. I took charge of the gauze pad that was put over her wound where her breast had been removed.

I remember she was very loving to me. She sang this song over me most nights:

> You are my sunshine my only sunshine,
> you make me happy when skies are gray.
> You'll never know dear, how much I love you,
> please don't take my sunshine away.

She would rub my temples, and I would fall asleep. But I could hear her saying to me, "When you grow up, you will be special." Her words were so important to me when, years later, enduring horrible verbal abuse on a daily basis—I was a terrible child, dumb, ugly, and just good for nothing—I would remember my mother's words, and they gave me the strength I needed.

CHAPTER 3

MY FATHER'S CONDITION

My father became very weak during this time. He was so heartbroken, watching his precious wife's health go downhill. He had problems with his heart, so he was also in and out of the hospital quite a bit.

Since my father was also in and out of the hospital, the Catholic Charities organization sent a very beautiful Black woman named Edda Long to be like a mom figure in our home. She did the cooking as well as watching over us children. We needed help, but she also gave us her love and her prayers.

Edda was a wonderful Christian woman, and I took to her like a mom. She would rock me to sleep at night and sing songs to me, then tuck me into bed. After I was in bed, she would go out to the hallway of our home, where she would cry and call upon the Lord. She lay on the floor asking God to have mercy on all of us children. She was such a wonderful Christian woman. At times she got loud, I would lay on my bed thinking, *Wow! God had better listen to her. She really means it.* Edda was a real prayer warrior, and I am grateful to this day for her prayers.

CHAPTER 4

THE PASSING AWAY OF MY PARENTS

The day finally came when my mom passed away, and Edda got us ready to go to the funeral. She reassured us that mother was in heaven, and we would see her again one day. We understood what she was saying, but my heart was broken. My father was still in the hospital, but our uncle told us that he would be home soon. We quickly learned he was just trying to reassure us.

When we got home from the funeral, I ran and got my crayons and paper so I could draw a picture for Daddy. I wrote "Welcome Home, Daddy" and put it on the front door. I made a second sign and ran to put one on his bedroom door.

A little while later the phone rang, and Edda answered it. She became very quiet and then took us into our parents' bedroom. We sat on the corner of the bed while Edda paced the floor. She started by reminding us that our mother was in heaven. We, of course, agreed with her and said we know we will see her again sometime. Then, with tears in her eyes, she told us that the good Lord had also taken our daddy to heaven.

I jumped up and started screaming, running to the front door telling Edda to see the picture I made that said "Welcome Home, Daddy."

We had to accept that both our parents were dead, Daddy had died on the same day as my mother's funeral. Still crying, I ran into my daddy's room and pulled all his suits off the hanger. I could still smell the Old Spice cologne that he wore. I thought if I lay there and cried he would come back. I cried my little heart out that day. I remember falling asleep. When I awoke, I felt peaceful and as if everything was going to be all right.

Many years later, I asked the Lord about that. He revealed that He heard Edda's prayers as she was praying in the hallway.

CHAPTER 5

OUR FIRST THREE MONTHS ALONE

Edda had to leave shortly after our parents passed away. I wanted her to stay with us, as she had seemed so much like my mom. She kept us safe and happy. We did survive alone, with my seventeen-year-old sister Kathy being like a parent to us. I remember eating spaghetti with butter and salt as our main meal.

At Christmas that year, our neighbors brought us some food and gifts. I recall getting a big doll and a pretty dress with colored bubbles all over the material. My brother got a bike and rode it around inside the house. They wished us a Merry Christmas and left. We were so happy that day because someone showed us they cared. Many years later, my husband and I sponsored families at Christmas time. Every time we brought gifts, it reminded me of my own experiences. I knew this would indeed bless them and make the children very happy.

One day, my brother and cousin went into a grocery store, filled up the cart and ran out of the store. We had food for a little while. To make money, we would go to the Arlington Racetrack and sell used programs.

Then a few days later, we went into a vacant house that was run down. We called it 'the old lady's house' because an old woman had lived there at one time, but the house was in no condition for anyone to live in. I remember going to the second floor, and it caved in. Miraculously, I was not hurt. It made us all laugh. My brother and cousins started kicking doors in. We all got bored and ran out of the place.

The next time we went to the store, a policeman was there, and he stared at us. He finally said, "I see you kids hanging around the track. You seem like you're nothing but trouble. I think I must talk to your parents. My brother said, "Well, we don't have any parents."

CHAPTER 6

THE COURTROOM

The authorities figured out where we lived and found out we were living by ourselves with no adult supervision. We had aunts and uncles, but none would take us in. When we were in the courtroom, our aunts and uncles debated which orphanage we should be sent to—the one in Chicago or the one in Michigan. Since they could not decide, the judge decided the one in Michigan would be the best choice.

As a child, I remember the feeling that nobody wanted us. Wow! They couldn't even agree on where to send us. Did anyone even care? I had mixed feelings at the time, and I'm sure my brothers and sisters must have felt the same way.

CHAPTER 7

ENTERING THE ORPHANAGE

The children's home in Michigan seemed like a long drive from Illinois. Everyone was very quiet the whole time we were traveling. I kept thinking about Edda and hoped there would be a lovely lady like her at the orphanage. When we got to the orphanage, our uncles and aunts said goodbye, and that was that. We never saw much of them after that. I lived in that orphanage for eleven years.

We were taken to the hospital located on campus when we arrived. We had a mini physical, and our blood type was put on a silver necklace that resembled a dog tag used in the military. Then we were taken to our new home.

Right away I could sense a cold and unloving environment. I had such a sick feeling in my heart. I knew, by the way the authorities acted toward us, that we were just a number, not real people. They never really talked with us after we were processed. We were driven to our so-called new home. They never even asked our names, much less where we were from. The people in charge acted just like robots.

CHAPTER 8

LIFE AT THE ORPHANAGE

They moved us around to different homes on campus. We started together in the same house, but eventually we were moved to different areas of the campus. So in the end, we did not get to live together for long. When all four of us were together at night, we could pray. My sister Kathy was the oldest and told us that we should pray the Lord's Prayer while we were together.

Shortly after that, we were separated, except my sister Sheila and I were kept together. I thank God for her. She saved my life, at least, twice. Our housemother was a very cold and heartless woman, and her only duties were ensuring we did our chores and had food, and that was all she did. The caretakers in charge did their jobs without concern about how we felt.

Sheila got to stay with me the longest. Usually, there were six to eight children per home with one housemother. The first night we were there, our housemother collected our pillows and put them in our closet. She said, "Rule #1 is that you do not get to sleep with your pillow." She declared that we would be punished if she caught us taking it out of the closet. She was so mean and harsh that I cried myself to sleep the first night, wishing Edda was here to sing me to sleep.

The housemother also seemed to single one other boy and me out from the rest, for whatever reason. She would let the others go outside but kept us inside. We had to sit in the basement. It was an old cellar-type basement that had dark concrete floors along with spiders—the typical Michigan cellar. It became clear that John and I were the two she hated more than the others.

She often let the others go to the Community Center but made us stay home. We had to hold a card table over our heads. Our arms would get shaky. She would crack our elbows with the end of the broomstick. At mealtime she served us food. We ate and would get full quickly, but her rule was to eat everything on your plate.

If we had poor table manners, she would have us hold our fingers up on the table so she could crack our knuckles with the end of a knife. Our little hands would go down, but she made us keep all our fingers up. She said, "I will not stop." I went to bed many evenings with sore elbows and sore knuckles.

At bedtime, she would have us line up in front of her and say, "Goodnight, Mother." I would cough when I said the word "mother" because she was not my mother. I knew that my real mother was very kind and loving. After saying goodnight to her, I would run upstairs to bed and try hard to remember all my mom's good words. She would tell me I would grow up to be special, and that I was a good little girl. She loved me, and I knew I would see her in heaven one day. I would remember Edda praying for all of us children, and I would go to bed remembering those good memories. It's what helped me cope with all the hostile surroundings that I faced daily.

We did not celebrate birthdays. For years at Christmas, we all got a box wrapped in brown paper with a box of chocolates, peanut brittle, and a few oranges. We were always thankful for what we received. Sometimes we would trade some of our items with each other. It is funny when I think about how, since I was so young, I learned to celebrate the smallest of things.

CHAPTER 9

TONSILS OUT

When I was about eleven-years-old, it was necessary for me to get my tonsils out. We had a small clinic on campus, but we were sent into town for surgery.

The doctor who did the surgery told me to eat Jello and pudding when I got home because my throat would be sore while it healed. The first night back home, I looked at the chili my housemother was serving up, I said. "Oh no, I can't eat that. The doctor said I should have Jello or pudding because my throat has to heal."

At that, she slammed her fist to the table and said loudly, "That doctor does not live here—you do. So you will follow my rules and eat that whole bowl of chili." She slid the bowl to where I was sitting at the table.

All the kids were looking at me, and two of them were crying. I rubbed my throat and ate chili one spoonful at a time. Each swallow hurt so badly.

She stared at me, and I kept going to prevent her from getting up and slapping me in the face. She had done that to us many times. I was afraid that her slap might hurt my throat even more.

I finished the bowl of chili and went to bed that night feeling very weak. My throat felt like it was on fire from all the rubbing with the food I was forced to eat.

It was about 2 o'clock in the morning and my nose was running, so I got up to get some tissue. I turned on the light and noticed blood coming from my nose. It was such a scary thing for me. I saw blood on the sheets and the floor from where I'd gone into the bathroom to get the tissue.

Instead of being concerned about all the blood I was losing, I was more afraid to ask my housemother to help, She would be mad at me because I messed up the sheets and the floor. I thought of my sister Sheila and knew she would not want me to bleed to death, so I did knock on my housemother's door and told her I needed some help.

When she saw the blood, she pushed me up against the wall and said, "What kind of a mess are you making?" She wrapped a large towel around my nose and mouth and made me clean up the floor with a rag. Then she made me rinse the sheets out and drape them over the shower stall.

The towel around my nose and mouth was getting red with blood. She called the transportation department on our campus, and they took me to the hospital in town.

The doctor said I was lucky I did not bleed to death. He looked me over, checking my throat. In an angry voice he said, "What did you eat for dinner?"

After I told him, he yelled, "I thought I told you to eat soft foods."

I told him my housemother's rules. He said that the rubbing of a meal of chili might be what caused the bleeding.

I left there feeling like such a bad kid and it must have been all my fault. It seemed like I could never do anything right.

My housemother not only physically abused me, but she also verbally abused me. That was even worse. She called me names and didn't ever call me by my real name. I thank God for the memories I had from my earlier years. I knew if my dad were here he would help me and probably go buy some Jello and pudding for me.

CHAPTER 10

THE STAIRCASE INCIDENT

I am thankful to God that my mind stayed clear. I also became a victim of much mental abuse. One of my chores was vacuuming the staircase with a small hand vacuum. When we got our chores finished we had to tell the housemother so she could check our work and see if it was done correctly.

While I was putting the vacuum cleaner away in the closet, she was busy going down the staircase sprinkling dust particles and little pieces of paper on the stairs. When I arrived at the bottom of the stairs where she stood, I asked her if everything was okay. She looked at me with such mean, ugly eyes she said, "You're a liar. You didn't vacuum these stairs. Look at the dust and the little papers on the stairs."

I was amazed because I knew I had done an excellent job, and nothing was there when I was done. She made me vacuum those stairs three times before she felt it was right. She wore an apron, and all the stuff on the stairs had come from her pocket. I was so young, and this was so confusing. I felt like I could never do anything good enough to please her.

CHAPTER 11

School Shopping

One day, a lady from the clothing department on campus invited a few girls to go school shopping in town. This was an event that did not happen often, so I was excited to be included. We mostly just wore clothes from the campus clothing store.

I don't know how I was asked to go, but I was very happy. I thought maybe I could pick out something special for school. There were ten of us going, and we each bought new sweaters. I got two skirts as well. My sweater was peach colored. I was also able to get slacks and shoes. I was amazed that my housemother let me go.

When I returned home, she told me to put all my clothes in her closet. It was about three weeks before school would start. I agreed and put them in her closet as directed. She said it in a lovely voice, which shocked me.

Two weeks later, she told me that her granddaughter was visiting from out of town. She was my age, and I was looking forward to meeting her. She came on a Saturday, and we seemed to hit it off immediately. We played jacks on the back porch and jumped rope. She was very nice. We were the same age and the same size.

My housemother called us in from outside, telling us she made a nice lunch. Before we went to eat, she told us to go into the living room.

We were very happy, laughing and having so much fun. I almost wish that she lived close to us. My housemother had a big box behind the chair. She started by telling her granddaughter that school would be starting very soon and told her she had some nice things to give her.

From the box, she pulled out a peach sweater. Looking at me, she said, "Look what grandma got you!"

It was my sweater! My heart just sank. She continued to bring out my skirts and other things. The saddest thing for me was, as she held up each item, she would deliberately hold them up in front of me, then she would turn to her granddaughter, handing them over to her.

It was as if she were saying to me "Ha ha. You can't do anything about this." Her granddaughter was so happy and thanked her.

My heart was broken, but I held back the tears. She had just given away all my new clothes to her granddaughter. Her granddaughter never knew, and I did not have the heart to tell her. She left after lunch with my clothes.

CHAPTER 12

RELIEF AT SCHOOL

When school started, I was so happy to get away from my sick home life for a few hours each day. The first morning she had us get up at five o'clock. That would be the regular routine.

We would sit on the stairs for an hour or more each morning until the bus came. I was in the sixth grade at the time. I was numb at school, and it was hard to focus because I knew what I'd be coming home to.

This went on for, at least, three more years. The abuse continued. We were locked in closets, and the maintenance man drilled holes in the bottom of the closet so we could breathe.

One time, my sister jumped on the back of the housemother and told her that she was tired of her beating on me. Sheila was even trying to punch her. She said, "How does that feel? Leave my little sister alone!" Then she ran up to the office on campus. She told the manager what was happening. He picked her up and gave her a spanking and told her to never come into his office and tell stories like that again.

I thank God for my sister Sheila who always tried to protect me. Sometimes the kids that lived there were bullies and beat up the younger kids. They tried it on me, and my sister punched several kids in the nose. She told them that if they ever thought about picking on her little sister, they would hear from her!

Many of the kids who were bullies were afraid of her. I never got bullied from any of the kids again after she had come to my rescue. One thing that I learned to do was survive and try to make the best of everything.

CHAPTER 13

MY MOVE ACROSS CAMPUS

My housemother was on a weekend break. The relief housemother got a call, and they told her I would be moving. She told me that I was being moved and to pack up my belongings as the van would be there in an hour.

I was so excited that I ran outside and did a flip, bumping my head on the bench. I thought, *Oh no. don't pass out! I'm going to be free today!* I didn't even care where I was moving. Anywhere on this campus would be better than this house—with this housemother.

The joy in my heart was so intense, I started singing while packing my belongings. It wasn't long before the van arrived to pick me up. I was overjoyed that my abusive housemother was not there. This meant I could leave in peace.

With a smile, the relief housemother said, "Goodbye and good luck."

Wow! That felt good! As I was being moved across campus, I got more and more excited. When the van dropped me off, I met the girls I would be living with.

They seemed like real sisters. My new housemother greeted me and said hello in a very pleasant voice. she instructed the girls to help me find my room.

My first evening meal made me feel like I had just left hell and entered heaven. My new housemother was a great cook. I was able to eat what I wanted. This housemother was a lovely lady, indeed. I could hardly believe that this new environment was possible. We still had chores to do and rules to follow, but they were all fair and reasonable. I enjoyed my new house and my new sisters, as we had a lot in common.

CHAPTER 14

DEATH OF MY HOUSEMOTHER

I was going to be entering high school in the fall. My sister Sheila was not living with me, as she was going to be a senior. We didn't see each other often. My older sister Kathy and brother Don had already left the orphanage. I felt so happy that I was moved, it enabled me to take deep breaths. I felt alive. I still had nightmares where my old housemother would make her way across campus just to hurt me. This lasted for the first few months.

I was playing catch with my neighbor when one of the kids approached me and told me that my old housemother was in the hospital, and she was really sick. I hadn't known that. The girl said she was asking about me and wanted to see me. I wondered what she wanted. Did she want to hit me one more time with the strength she had left?

I told them I didn't want to go see her. Thanks anyway. The next day someone else found me and told me that her nurse had asked them to have me come see her. I realized I was much more secure and smarter and could handle her. If she started something, I could easily hold my own with her.

I made my way up to the hospital on campus where she was. I stood at the end of her bed, and with a very sarcastic tone, I said, "Somebody said you wanted to see me. Even if you move toward me, I will punch the daylights out of you. I'm bigger and wiser now."

She looked over at me with tears in her eyes, trying to raise her body from the bed. She could hardly get the words out. She said, "Diane, will you ever forgive me for what I've done to you?" She was halfway up in the bed, looking shaky and white as a ghost.

I quickly responded, "Yes." I thought she might die right there. I surely didn't mean it at the time. I left there just numb. She had hurt me so badly during my childhood that I just wanted to get out of there. I was glad to start a new life, knowing she would not be a part of it.

About a week later, a neighbor kid came running by and told me that she had died. I must admit, I felt such relief surround me from head to toe. She could never hurt me again. I was happy that this put closure on the nightmare life I had while living under her reign for seven and a half years.

CHAPTER 15

High School

When I entered high school, I didn't realize the awesome abilities I had. I had been told so often that I was no good, I believed it

I found I was gifted with athletics, which showed when I tried out for Track and Field. My sister Sheila was in the twelfth grade, and I just entered ninth grade. We were both on the Track Team, placing first in most events.

At one track meet, I entered five events and placed first in all events but one, in which I placed second. I competed in the Triple Jump, High Jump, 440 Relay, 75-Yard Dash, and the 50-Low Hurdles. My sister and I even held some school records.

My new housemother gave me space to grow. I was able to make good decisions on my own. I also tried out for cheerleader and made varsity in the tenth grade.

I did enjoy my high school years. For a while, I could put all the bad treatment I had to deal with when I was younger out of my mind. When I participated in track and field, I would think of my dad. All my friends had parents that would be cheering them on. I just looked up to the sky, knowing my dad was watching. I remembered what he said when I was five, "My little girl is a strong runner."

At the children's home when you graduate from high school, it is mandatory that you leave immediately. So on the very day of my graduation, instead of a celebration, I had my bags packed and ready to go. My housemother had reminded me to be ready to go after graduation because transportation would pick me up.

We had no one celebrating with us when we walked across the stage to pick up our diplomas. As soon as we received our diplomas we had to go home, put our cap and gown on the chair, get our suitcase, and leave.

When I look back, it seemed that graduation should be a wonderful day to leave a place you did not like. However, leaving with no sense of direction was scary. I had not been prepared for the outside world.

CHAPTER 16

ADVENTURE TO THE OUTSIDE WORLD

I walked out the door homeless, with no driver's license, and no knowledge of cooking or buying groceries.

We were never allowed to cook, and the groceries were always delivered to the house. I was emotionally unprepared for the outside world. Instead, I was very good at putting on a mask and pretending everything was all right, even if it was not. I had learned how to cope with my situation.

Before I walked out the door, the housemother said an envelope was on the desk for me. Thinking it was just a card, I slipped the envelope into my pocket to look at later. I smiled as she told me goodbye and wished me good luck.

My friend Jenny told me I could spend one night at her house. When we arrived at her home, I met her parents and they were very nice to me. I thought, this is what a real family feels like.

Her parents had called her into another room. As I sat there, I remembered putting the envelope into my pocket. I took out the envelope, opened it, and was amazed to find a check for almost $4000. I was shocked! I couldn't think of where this had come from.

Jenny came back into the room and announced that her parents wanted to send her to Hawaii. She would be able to see her boyfriend, who would be there for R&R from Vietnam. She asked if I would like to come. I had just seen the check, and I knew that I could afford to go, so why not? I told her I would love to go with her.

She packed her bags, and before we knew it we were on the way to the airport. What a great graduation gift! A trip to Hawaii! I believe that the Lord was truly blessing me. I felt like a bird just being let out of a cage. The plane ride was fun and exciting. Her parents had arranged for us to stay at a lovely place while we were there.

CHAPTER 17

MY FRIEND MET HER BOYFRIEND

My friend went to where families visited the military men and women on R&R. While she was there, I walked to the beach feeling like I had just landed in heaven. It was beautiful there, and I even took a surfing class. One night we went to a restaurant with an attached nightclub where there was dancing. Jenny saw a poster that was advertising a dance contest. She felt that I was a terrific dancer and told me I should enter the contest. That made me laugh.

A few nights later we had decided to return to the same restaurant. I was watching people dance when I noticed a young man whose style was much like mine. Again, Jenny insisted that I join the dance contest. She said that maybe that guy could be my dance partner. Before the night was over, I had introduced myself to him. He asked me to be his dance partner for the contest. I thought it would be fun, so I agreed.

I did not realize it at the time, but the contest we signed up for was the Hawaii State Dance Championship for 1970. We found a place where we could practice our dance moves. What set us apart was our ability to do jumps and cartwheels—a form of break dancing. We were truly ahead of our time. Break dancing did not become popular until many years later.

We went to a store and bought awesome costumes. They were a shimmery blue color. The tops were tight on the arms with big material halfway up. Believe it or not, this was a popular look for the 60s and 70s. We also had bell bottom slacks and high platform boots. We put in a lot of practice time. We practiced in our costumes as well.

We heard that there were salsa dancers, ballroom dancers, and even Hawaiian dancers who would be competing against us. When the dancing began, several couples were performing at the same time.

As the eliminations progressed, the number of groups got smaller and smaller. We were still in the competition and had progressed to the point where there were only three couples left—the Salsa dancers, the Hawaiian dancers, and the Break dancers (that was us). They eliminated the Salsa dancers, leaving only the Hawaiian dancers and us.

I thought for sure the Hawaiian dancers would win. Finally, the announcement was made that the Hawaiian 1970 State Dance Champions are Robert and Diane, the modern dancers! Wow! We screamed with excitement and joy, we were both so delighted. We each received a large trophy to keep, a cash prize, and for a year, everything was free at any restaurant or nightclub on the island. I just could not believe the blessings that had come our way.

We went out to dinner to celebrate. And because it was free, we ordered steaks. My friend Jenny and I loved

Hawaii so much at that point, we decided to live there and get jobs. We lived there for nine months.

CHAPTER 18

TIME TO THINK ABOUT THE FUTURE

The experience of Hawaii was awesome, but I decided it was time to think about my future. In high school, I liked drama class and was in a number of plays. I remembered that the children's home where I grew up said if I wanted further education, they had funding to help me.

I decided to go to New York to investigate a possible acting career. I rented a room at the YMCA and inquired about acting schools during the day, I finally found one in Carnegie Hall, called the Dramatic Workshop. The school was college-level and taught acting and speech classes. I got ahold of the children's home administration, and they agreed to pay for the classes.

I also worked part time at Amory Theater and enrolled as a student at the New York Karate Academy. I enjoyed the karate classes—I think it was good for me physically and emotionally. I was able to take out some inner frustrations in a positive way.

One day, my instructor was asked by a film company making a martial arts film, if he knew any students who would want to have a small part in his movie, someone who knew fighting techniques. My instructor picked a few of us to try out. Of course, we all said yes! I was very excited to be part of the film, even though I had little experience in acting. The filming for the movie was done on a weekend, so it worked out well with my schedule. I enjoyed my acting classes, and I tried out for a few plays in New York, but nothing worked out for me.

CHAPTER 19

DIANE WITH THE CIRCUS

One day our acting teacher mentioned there was a bulletin board with auditions listed on it, including anything from commercials to small parts in film. After class, I checked out the bulletin board's listings.

I noticed that the Ringling Brothers and Barnum and Bailey circus were having auditions at Madison Square Garden. There would also be dance auditions for aerial ballet. Since I was good at athletics, I thought I could climb a rope and do aerial ballet.

When I arrived at the audition, I saw many young women with tight buns on their heads and ballet costumes. I didn't know if this would work for me. I hadn't trained in ballet. I remember my acting coach telling us to just try out for anything—doing so could lead to something else. So I stayed.

The choreographer had us go out in threes before he called us up. He had us follow his lead with a dance routine. My turn came and I remembered all the moves. I felt pretty good when I left.

I didn't think much of it afterwards. I just continued taking classes in both acting and martial arts and completed my Brown Belt in Karate. About three weeks later, I got a notice in the mail from Ringling Brothers Circus that I had been selected as a showgirl. I was to report to training headquarters in Sarasota, Florida.

I was surprised, as I had said I would do aerial ballet and ride elephants. Before I knew it, I was in Florida at the training grounds. I signed the contract, and a lovely person showed me where I would live. I lived on a train in a tiny little room with a big window. The guide showed me where the animal, clown, and aerobics train cars were. It was a long train, containing all different acts, and the animals traveled with the circus in their own cars.

That evening, we all met in the auditorium where the training would take place. The director greeted us and explained the schedule, which would start the next day.

I looked around and was amazed at the number of people that it took to assemble their performances. There were several performers from other countries. I looked at someone with clown makeup and thought it was a toddler. Then I heard someone who said, "This is Vinhio, the smallest man in the world." I laughed as I looked around and saw people from all walks of life. I thought, "This was now my new family." I wasn't nervous. I felt like I would fit right in.

We started our training early the following day. I worked hard at what I did. The job wasn't easy, but I was glad I had training in martial arts. I knew I had the strength to climb a rope sixty-feet up in the air and hang with one foot in a small opening at the top. They also trained us to swing around very fast. I thought I would get dizzy, but we were instructed to look at one object while spinning. Surprisingly, that trick made the difference.

Getting on an elephant was my other job. My elephant's name was Toby. The animal trainer showed us how to put our foot on the elephant's leg, and say "Toby, up!" and whipped his leg hard, and just like that ... I was on top of him!

It was so much fun learning everything I was going to do. I did aerial ballet and dance productions and rode the elephants. After the training, we were given a break for two weeks. After our break, we would start performing in Florida. I also signed up to go to Europe. I would be gone for a year, constantly on the move. The circus I worked for was billed as the Greatest Show on Earth. This sounded cool and adventurous to me. During the break, I returned to Michigan to see my sister Sheila. I wanted her to know that I would be gone for a year.

Many years later, I was visiting the Mega Mall in DeWitt, Michigan, and I found one of the programs from the show where I was performing with the circus. This is what Rich Kelly, owner of the mall, said about my experience.

"I absolutely love that the Mega Mall has been credited for people unearthing many amazing relics. Some are incredibly valuable in a monetary sense, and some are incredibly valued to only the customers. Over the years, we have heard countless testimonies from our customers about these rare and joyous fines. But none have exceeded what Diane Dalton and her husband found while stopping at the Mega Mall for the first time. A 1974 program of the Ringling Brother's Barnum and Bailey Circus with her picture on it! How cool is that? A $10 item to the rest of us, priceless to her. Diane was a showgirl for the circus, dangling in the air by her ankle, and riding the magnificent elephants. She was so incredibly surprised and thankful to find this treasure at our Mega Mall. And we thank you, Diane, for helping to bring such everlasting memories to all of us!"

Paul and I were absolutely delighted to find this program so many years later.

PICTURE OF DIANE ON HER ELEPHANT TOBY

PICTURE OF DIANE AS ARIAL ARTIST

CHAPTER 20

PAUL AND I MEET

My sister Sheila lived in Lansing, Michigan, in an apartment complex. One day I was outside playing with her son, who was five-years-old at the time. I saw a person out of the corner of my eye walking toward the trash container. I looked up as he walked by. He was very muscular and handsome. Bleach-blond hair and a fantastic tan.

He turned our way and said, "Hi. I'm Paul, the manager of the apartments. Are you visiting?"

"Yes, I am."

"Maybe I'll see you around. Have a nice day." And he walked away.

I guess I was not very friendly, as I had a chip on my shoulder. I thought, "Oh well, I'll be leaving soon. I probably won't ever see him again anyway."

The next day, I went grocery shopping with my sister, and when we came back to her apartment, Paul was nearby. He asked if he could help bring in our groceries, and Sheila said, "Yes, thank you." After all the groceries were brought in, Paul and I started to talk.

Paul mentioned that he had studied martial arts. My wall came down when he said that because I was also taking martial arts classes. We walked together around the apartment complex, having a pleasant conversation. The topic was mainly karate and the different styles of martial arts.

Paul changed the subject and told me he had found faith in Jesus Christ. He said he really liked going to church. He told me that if I didn't know what direction to go in life, all I had to do was just ask Jesus and He would show me. I put his words in my heart that day and have kept them close—even today.

CHAPTER 21

My Return to the Circus

I enjoyed my visit with my sister, but it was time to go back to the circus. I went back to Florida because my performances would start soon. I still had a lot of practice and rehearsal time before we opened our first show in Miami.

I went to a local Kmart store, bought a picture of Jesus, and put it in my room on the train. I looked at it daily and asked Jesus to please show me what He wanted me to do with my life. I was hoping to stay a whole year with the circus, but I also knew this would not be a lifelong career. I remembered what Paul told me to ask Jesus, so I did just that. I didn't know Jesus yet, but looking at His picture and asking Him that question made me feel like I was accomplishing something.

It was fun looking out my window as the train traveled to different places. The opening show was a great success. Young women on the train talked about the men from Bulgaria, a teeter board act. Sometimes they drank alcohol and the girls would get very scared.

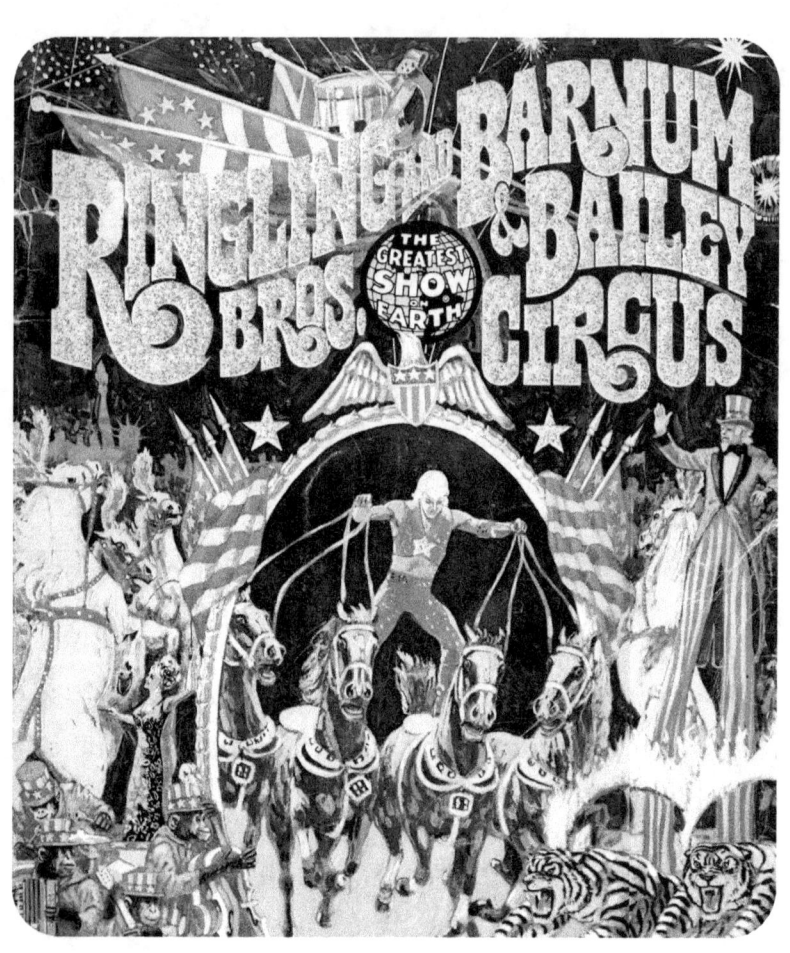

CHAPTER 22

DANGER ON THE TRAIN

One Sunday, we were all in our rooms, and a loud banging on the door startled everyone.

Suddenly, the door was pushed open! I heard girls screaming in terror. Then someone said, "Go get that girl who knows karate. She needs to help us."

At that point I thought of Paul, who was a black belt in karate, but Paul was not here with me. I looked at my picture of Jesus and said, "If You're real, please help me."

When I opened my door, men were coming down the hallway. One man was muscular. He was the one that held three people on his shoulders in the act. The other one was smaller but robust.

They had a crazy look in their eyes and smelled like alcohol. All I remember was walking toward them with authority, pointing at them, and telling them to get off the train right then.

They looked at me and seemed so afraid, they turned around and ran so fast they tripped over each other. They picked themselves up and ran away from the train.

I went back to my room, looked at my picture of Jesus, and said, "I know You are real."

All the girls were clapping and cheering for me, but I knew the Lord had sent angels to stand behind me because of the look in the men's eyes. I knew it wasn't me but something more significant that caused them to leave immediately.

This incident truly helped me believe that there was something about Jesus that I wanted desperately. I continued to pray every morning, asking Jesus what He wanted me to do with my life.

We toured other cities in Florida, and I was enjoying myself, getting into the routine. A few months later, I was on my elephant, Toby. The music was playing *God Bless America*. We always wore glittering costumes, and the elephants had headpieces and were draped with red, white, and blue. This was called the Spectacular Number. The elephants would go around the three rings with the music playing *God Bless America*. This was the day I decided to talk with Jesus.

CHAPTER 23

Jesus Talks to Me

I had been looking at my picture of Jesus for months and daily asked what He wanted me to do with my life.

One day, He spoke to me as I was on top of Toby, waving to the crowd. There were thousands of people in the arena, enjoying all the glitter and glamour of the circus.

Suddenly, the Lord spoke to my heart and said, "Diane, keep waving. You're saying goodbye to this world." It was almost an audible voice, it was so clear and loud enough for me to hear over all the noise.

I answered Him as I was waving, "Okay, I'm saying goodbye. But where am I going?" He answered me again! "I want you to go back to Michigan tomorrow at 5:00 a.m." That's all I heard. I had no idea what would come from that, but I heard it so clearly.

So, that day when we finished the show, I took off my costume for the last time and took it to the costume lady. When I told her goodbye, she said, "No, I'll see you tomorrow for the show."

I said, "No, I'm going to a whole new world."

She looked at me, smiled, and said, "Okay."

I went back to my room and sat down, thinking about all that happened that evening. I knew I had heard Jesus clearly, so I packed my bag. I went to bed a little early because He had said to leave at five o'clock in the morning. I felt that I should follow His directions completely.

I got up without even an alarm clock that morning at approximately 4:15 a.m. I walked off the train at 5:00 a.m. The cleaning lady was there and asked me where I was going. I told her it was hard to explain, but I had to go back to Michigan and to let everyone know I was okay, but I had a family emergency. She said she would let them know.

Then I walked down the train, passing all the other train cars, the animals, and the clown cars. I knew it had to be God because, as much fun as I was having, I wasn't sad to leave. I knew it was God's timing.

I found a taxi, took it to the airport, and flew back to Michigan. When I got off the plane, Michigan felt rather cold, as I was used to the Florida weather. I asked Jesus what to do next. I didn't hear anything, so I called my sister. She had a friend pick me up and bring me to her house.

CHAPTER 24

FOLLOWED THE TRUE PATH

The following day, I tried to tell my sister what happened, but she didn't quite understand what I was talking about. She gave me Paul's phone number.

I called him, and I asked if he remembered some months ago when he had said that if I wasn't sure what to do with my life, just ask Jesus and He'd show me. I told him I think Jesus showed me what I should do, and now I'm back from Florida. So I asked Paul what I should do now.

Little did I know that Paul's Bible study had been praying for me for the months I was away. He had spoken to his pastor about feeling that God was calling him to marriage.

The only girl he could think about was hanging 60-feet in the air and riding elephants while traveling with the circus. He asked the pastor if he should forget about her or could that be what God wanted him to do. His pastor told him they would pray about it every Tuesday during Bible study. If it was God's will, He would bring her back to Michigan.

So, Paul asked me to come to the Tuesday night Bible study. I showed up there, and when I knocked on the door, I introduced myself. The lady who answered the door said, "Oh my word! We've been praying for you." I didn't quite understand how all that worked, but I thanked her. That night I asked Jesus to come into my heart. It was then I began to understand that He was the Way, the Truth, and the Life.

I saw such joy in the people there. They were so kind and loving. I knew the love I experienced there must come from someplace other than human kindness.

The pastor and his wife asked me where I would be staying. I told them that I didn't know. I didn't have any big plans. They offered me a bed in their basement if I would like. They said I was welcome to live with them. I took them up on their offer. It was a beautiful experience for me. The couple were very godly people.

Mary taught me a lot about cooking and taking care of children. I thought if I could be anything like her, that would be great. I quickly learned domestic skills I hadn't learned when I was in the children's home. It was very exciting for me to be around loving and kind people. I saw what a real family looked like.

This was an enjoyable time in my life. For the next six months, Paul and I would go to church together and attend Bible study. We became great friends. Paul taught me that reading my Bible and praying would help me know Jesus more and more. The pastor and his wife, who were very kind people, showed me a lot about family life.

One night, I dreamed I was following Paul through a maze at the playground. I was following him and then suddenly I lost track of where he went. When I woke up from the dream, my heart was pounding. I asked myself what this was. I felt the Lord put in my heart that when I followed Paul, I would know where I was going. But when I lost track of him I wouldn't be sure, because that's the man He wanted me to marry.

I kept it in my heart, but I knew God had spoken to me and told me that we should be married. Paul revealed that he, too, had a dream. In the dream, he got a hard nudge on his side that woke him up. He felt the Lord's presence telling him to take care of me. We dated for about six months and then we got married.

PAUL AND DIANE'S WEDDING PICTURE

CHAPTER 25

LIFE'S REFLECTION

I never even saw myself living past twenty-five-years old. I never saw any hope for my future growing up, as I had lived with so much rejection and fear of failure. But I knew I loved Paul, and I loved the fact that he loved the Lord.

We got married and lived in East Lansing, Michigan. He went with me for my first trip to the grocery store. It was the first time I had been in a grocery store where you buy groceries, bring them home, and then cook food. Again, this was because in the children's home we weren't allowed to cook, and the grocery store delivered the food to our house.

When we walked into the store, I felt embarrassed because I knew I didn't know what I was doing. Paul was so patient and kind to me. He realized that I was coming from a dark place with no hope. It is funny when we look back on that day, but I was amazed at all the food.

When we finished our shopping and came home. I had to tell him that I had only a few cooking skills.

CHAPTER 26

EARLY YEARS OF OUR MARRIAGE

Embarrassed to admit to my very few cooking skills, I started crying. But Paul had grown up on a farm and had many opportunities to help cook. He comes from a family of five children, and even used to cook for the hired hands that worked on the farm.

He was so kind and would help me. We learned together, and I became an excellent cook. I even made homemade bread! We were a young couple, learning about life. Sometimes, he was more like a father to me than a husband because I was emotionally still young in heart. I had to have inner healing take place.

I got pregnant not long after we were married. I was so happy to be pregnant, to have a child. I hadn't thought I would ever have that in my life. I was so excited to be having a child. We attended a close-knit church, and some of the ladies of the church had maternity clothes that I could use. My pregnancy went well, and my first daughter was born.

We really enjoyed our family. About a year and a half later we had our second child. We went on to have five children. Paul and I stayed active in the church. We took our children to the childcare, where they learned about Jesus.

It was the most thrilling time in my life because I felt like God was restoring me, giving me a family I never had. His Word says He is a father to the fatherless. I felt like He fathered me and completely restored me. It was almost like He was saying that He knew I didn't have a good family life growing up, but He would create a beautiful family for me. He did restore back all those years that were lost, and we so enjoyed our family.

THE DALTON'S FIVE YOUNG CHILDREN

CHAPTER 27

CHAMPION'S CLUB

Paul was a good plumber and heating contractor. His business provided a good income for our family. As our children got older, I realized I had an urge to help heartbroken people. I wanted to help those less fortunate because I had grown up in an environment where there wasn't much love.

At the time, I became a part of our church's ministry called Champions Club. They sent buses around the lower income housing developments throughout our city. The buses brought in children on Saturdays for what they called Saturday Church.

When the children came running to the bus, I would get so excited to see their smiling faces. Some would come running with their pajamas still on because they didn't want to miss the bus. I knew some of them were living without fathers in the home. I saw how important it was to show the love of God to these children. So that was the start of my ministry work. I continued to be involved in this ministry for many years.

God says in His Word that He comes to heal the broken hearted. I was thrilled to be a part of His healing process for the children we picked up each week.

As Christians, we should be the light and the salt of the earth wherever we go. I enjoyed Champions Club, and we did it for a good number of years. In the summer, we would go out with a truck we called Sidewalk Sunday school. We went into the neighborhoods and pulled the side of the truck down to become a stage. We would do puppet shows and children's ministries for the kids. We put a massive tarp out on the grass, and kids would come from all over. We would hand out treats and snacks while the kids listened to the stories we shared.

We also got to know the moms—helped some of them who were struggling with drugs and financial problems. We connected them to various resources and walked them through getting the help they needed. It was very rewarding to watch these families come to know Jesus through the love and kindness the Champions Club ministry showed them.

We had some 13- and 14-year-old children come by our truck asking when we would have something for them. They were getting older, now teenagers. I was asked to start a ministry that we called Life Club. It was for children 13 to 19 years of age. We ran it pretty much the same way as we did for the younger children, except the bus ran on Fridays at 6:00 p.m. It was interesting and very rewarding. But we would have teenagers fighting on the bus. It was a real challenge, but we pressed through it. It was hard to find volunteers for that ministry because many people didn't want to be around all the chaos.

But life is exciting when God calls you to do something. I always had my ears inclined to the Lord, and that gave me the wisdom to be a good mom. He also gave me the insight to know how to be a good wife. Now He would provide me with the knowledge to become a good minister of the good news of the gospel to these teenagers.

Like the younger kids, many of them came from fatherless homes. Many of them had been in and out of the juvenile system. But we were able to be like a neon light, pointing them to Jesus. Many of the teens turned things around and became helpers with the ministry, which was a gratifying experience.

DIANE AND A BUNCH OF KIDS IN A YARD

KIDS AND DIANE ON A BACK PORCH

CHAPTER 28

YOUTH MINISTRY

I also became the youth minister at Mount Hope Church in the City in Lansing, Michigan. We had a van designated to pick up the kids. But within a very short period, we went from that van to a bus and ended up with sixty teenagers in our ministry. But as I mentioned, ministering to that age group became chaotic.

One time, a bus driver got upset because these kids were so unruly. She put the bus in park and said she didn't think she could do this anymore. She said she thought the kids were crazy and I was crazy, and she was done. She got off the bus. We weren't even in the church parking lot!

I remember those days, and I knew that God was not telling me to quit. That bus driver eventually came back. She said the Lord told her to come back and, at least, get the bus to the parking lot this time.

Because of the chaotic nature of Life Club, some volunteers would leave the ministry. But I wouldn't quit until God said to quit. It's really rewarding when we do what God asks us to do. Every now and then I'll see some of the kids I worked with. They're now in their 30s and have families. They come and thank me for loving them when no one else would. This was an extremely rewarding time of ministry.

We also had a soup kitchen at our church. We would reach out to the homeless, but not only to feed them. We would have coat drives so we were able to give them coats, hats, and gloves, which would put a smile on people's face. Michigan can become bitter cold in the winter and very dangerous to the homeless.

One time there was a couple that came to the soup kitchen, and they both had colds. They had runny noses because they had to sleep outside. They told me they found a dumpster with shredded paper inside where they slept at night to stay warm.

A friend had given me a beautiful comforter about a month earlier that she wanted to donate. I was hoping to give it to someone who needed it. I knew, at the right time, God would show me who to give it to.

The couple came in to have a free dinner that we were serving at the soup kitchen. Afterward, we had coffee, and I talked to them. They told me how cold they got at night.

I felt the Lord say to give them the beautiful comforter. When I brought it out, they asked if I was sure I wanted to give it to them. They stuffed the blanket in their bag and thanked me.

A short time later, they came back to the soup kitchen. They were so happy. They wanted to thank me for the blanket because, shortly after I gave it to them, they were able to get a room to rent. They called it the Jesus blanket. It meant a lot to them. It was such a beautiful blanket, they knew that, indeed, it came from the Lord. They felt like they were royal children of the King of kings every time they made the bed.

Another time, a lady came that was a prostitute. She would use our bathroom to change her clothes. I knew what she was doing. When she came out of the bathroom, she would go behind the clothing room that we had and fall asleep. I would let her stay in there and sleep.

One day, at the prompting of the Lord, I went around the side to the clothing area and told her to wake up. She sat up quickly and asked what's going on. She was a little bit irritated. I told her we had been letting her come in and sleep, and we didn't mind, but today the Lord told me to talk to her. So I told her that if she didn't change her ways, somebody's going to ask me to come and identify an unknown body behind the dumpster. I didn't want that to be her.

I didn't know what she had been doing, but I wanted to help her. She started crying and told me there was a warrant out for her arrest, and she was scared. She didn't know how to deal with it. She had already been to prison and was out on parole. She said if she got in trouble again, she would probably have to go back to prison.

I called her parole officer, and the lady told us both to come and see her. The parol officer told her that if she would just turn herself into Ingham County Jail, she didn't think she would have to return to prison. But, she said that she had to take care of this, or she probably would end up there.

I was willing to take the church van and drive her to the jail. She agreed, even though she was hesitant at first. When we stopped to get gas, she started to walk off.

I stopped her and told her we were going to do this. Come to find out, she only had to serve three months. After she served her three months, we found a rehabilitation program in Grand Rapids that she could go to get some help with her drug use.

She lived there for a year and turned her life around. She was a different person and had such love and joy for Jesus. It was a true blessing to see how her life was transformed.

CHAPTER 29

OUR MINISTRY—A BLESSING TO MANY

We had many opportunities to minister to people that came to our soup kitchen. In our youth ministry, we had one young man whose mother was a crack cocaine addict. Her name was Angel. He was so afraid that she was going to die. So, on our Friday ministry nights, we would pray for her.

After a few months, she called me and wanted to know what was happening with her son, Steve. I told her he seems to be enjoying the youth program. He likes to play basketball, and he gets along with everybody.

She said she didn't mean anything like that. She said he told her that his group had been praying for her. Ever since he's been doing that, I've lost my desire for drugs. She couldn't believe it! It was a miracle! And she asked if she could please get on that bus and see what this youth group does.

I told her she was more than welcome. She started getting on the bus every Friday night and started to help us. We had a big celebration party. We got her our T-shirt and a CD, and even gave her a brand-new Bible. I saw her about a year later. She told me she was drug free and thanked our program. She said she was so glad that we told her and her son about Jesus.

CHAPTER 30

THE HOUSE OF HOPE

We continued to develop and be a part of other ministries. I will say, when God is healing your broken heart, it leaves you willing to tell others the good news. God can heal and restore your life, pick up the broken pieces and put your life back together, better than you were before your difficulties and hurt. That is God's way.

BROKEN BUT FIXED

I was asked to become a youth pastor in a ministry called the House of Hope. The "house" was really not much more than a garage. In the backyard, there was a slab of concrete and a torn basketball hoop. The house was located in the middle of a very rough neighborhood. Drugs were being sold on the corner. We were used to shootings, and fights were common in that neighborhood. I thought that the house would be a good place to put a pool table. My friend brought a pool table, and with the help from others, we set it up. We also fixed the basketball net. I prayed for guidance on how to get the youth to come in.

One of the ways we got them to come was when we advertised we were holding a pool tournament, and the cash prize was $200. We took flyers to a high school near our newly founded center. After school, we passed out a ton of flyers to the students as they were leaving the school. The flyers also mentioned there would be free pizza and soft drinks. God knew that was just the right combination to bring out the teens in our area. And boy, did they come!

Youth Pool Tournament

The house was filled with teenagers, very eager to participate in the pool tournament. We figured out how many games to play and how to have a playoff. We had them all sit down so we could explain the rules. They all cheered when we announced that the winner would receive $200. We spoke to them for a few minutes to make them feel welcome. I let them know that God loved them, and He had a great plan for their future.

BROKEN BUT FIXED

KIDS IN THE YARD WITH A BIG GREEN FROG

OLDER KIDS IN HOUSE WITH HEADS BOWED IN PRAYER

CHAPTER 31

THE JESUS GANG

The event proved to be a great success. It was two o'clock in the morning before the winner was announced. I was tired but happy to see so many having a good time and not on the streets getting into trouble.

We had invited many teenagers from the area and found that we were always packed on Friday nights. There was a halfway house down the street for young men coming out of juvenile prison. I taught a Bible study there on Wednesdays. Some of those young men became reliable helpers. Some even followed me to the other ministries, and I found that I could depend on them.

They spoke to the youth and gave testimonies of their experiences. I truly believe that some of the kids listened and learned that the choices they make today would determine where they would end up tomorrow.

We shared Jesus Christ with them, that He was a personal savior and their only hope. Each week we had many teenagers who came to the Lord and were saved. They in turn spoke to their friends and families. One young teen suggested we call our Friday night bunch, the Jesus Gang. He told us that he could go to the dope houses, but he chose to go to the house of God—known as the House of Hope. The ministry was remarkably successful, and we saw many lives changed.

OUTREACH FOR OLDER TEENS AND YOUNG ADULTS
IN BACK YARD

Younger kids being taught by the olders

DIANE BAPTIZING A MAN

CHAPTER 32

FOOD MINISTRY

We had block parties and invited family and friends from the whole neighborhood. Others may tell you this is not possible, but one can do missions work in their own hometown.

A friend of mine who owned a restaurant had a tragedy in his family, when a family member took their own life. One day, he noticed six men on the corner. He stopped to ask them if they were hungry. They all said yes, so he got them some sandwiches. That was such a simple thing to do for those who are on the streets.

This is how his street ministry began. Jesus told us to feed the hungry. We got permission to use a parking lot area and brought meals. There were volunteer food handlers and helpers. We all showed up, even in the winter.

My friend was getting ready to move and asked if I would take over that food ministry. We got permission to use the inside of the building, which made it somewhat easier. Michigan winters are very cold, it seemed fitting to bring the ministry inside. We would have a short message and then serve the food. We served from 75 to 100 people every Tuesday. We heard people say they used to come just for the food, but now they came to hear the Word of God. We drove many to Teen Challenge, helped others get jobs, and drove others to the mental health checkups they needed. We gave out clothes and other personal items to those who needed them.

For those who got apartments, we would bless their home and help them with pots and pans, towels and … the basics. And we included a bag of groceries. This act of kindness helped many to stay in their apartments. They became disciplined enough to keep their jobs.

This building of hope became the Church, keeping many of them off the streets. It was a way to help those who were on drugs and alcohol. Many were saved, being born again, and filled with the Holy Spirit. We used a big water trough to do baptisms. They became workers for God, each in their own way.

CHAPTER 33

THE TESTIMONY OF MATT

There was a man named Matt who drank alcohol every day. One night he came to dinner and asked if he could talk to me. He started crying and said he missed his children and his ex-wife. They lived in another town a few hours away. He said he was ready to ask them to forgive him for neglecting them for so many years.

My friend and I told him we would pay for his bus ticket if he would meet us at the bus station the next morning at 8:00 o'clock. He did show up, and we had his ticket and a bag of snacks for his trip. We prayed for him and waved as the bus pulled away.

A few weeks later he came back. He was so excited. He said, since we prayed for him about his drinking, he was down to one beer a day. And when he asked his family to forgive him, they did! He now had a job painting and was going to move back home in the next week. He had been homeless and so broken.

Sometimes, just showing love to people can inspire them to take the next step.

CHAPTER 34

DESPERATION OF HOMELESS MEN

Another homeless man came to our free dinner sponsored by our Into the Streets Ministry. He declared that he was going to run into the street and have a car hit him. He wanted to die. He started to run toward the traffic, and two of our volunteers grabbed him and brought him back into the building. He passed out, and we called 911. The ambulance came and took him to the hospital.

My husband Paul and I followed behind the ambulance. We talked to a nurse and asked her how he was doing. She said that normally they let people sleep a while and then release them; especially if they're homeless.

I asked if I could talk to a doctor. The doctor came down the hall, and first he asked how we were related to this person. I told him I was a minister that oversees the street ministry. The man was one who came to our free dinners each week.

I told the doctor that he was suicidal and needed help. I thank God, because that doctor gave me permission to sign a paper that would get him into a program to help him with drugs and alcohol.

I saw him a year later at the bus station. He came running up to me, thanking me for helping him get the help he needed. The program he was sent to changed his life. He said he was now doing good, had a job, and was free from all drugs and alcohol. We had the privilege of watching people change as they received Jesus, watching them get back on their feet was always a great reward for Paul and me.

CHAPTER 35

PAUL HELPED TO MINISTER

It always amazes me how just showing that you care, with the love of Jesus guiding you, people can change. The Holy Spirit guides them to a better plan. We are just instruments in God's hands.

My husband Paul would ask the people who were at our free dinner if any of them wanted to work the next day. There were always a few who did want to work. He would pick them up and take them to his work site, where they did manual labor required with the plumbing jobs.

Some of the workers had been in and out of prison and were homeless. Many just wanted to work to make a day's wage and feel better about themselves. Paul helped them to get on their feet, and he even directed them to other places that were hiring workers for regular jobs. He never judged anyone. He just showed God's love, and they all respected and appreciated him.

CHAPTER 36

THE STOLEN BIKE

We had a young man named Marcus come in with his bike. He asked if he could keep it in the building while he had his dinner. We said that would be okay, but about a half hour later, an older man came into the building shouting and screaming at the top of his lungs, saying every curse word possible.

He saw Marcus with the bike near him and shouted that the young man had stolen his son's bike. He started to get physical with him. Paul stepped in and explained that we had let him come in with the bike because we thought it was his. The man grabbed the bike, cursed again at Marcus, then left.

We prayed about this situation, and Paul and I felt this would be a good time to show the love and mercy of God.

The next time Marcus came to our program, I sat down with him and got to know him a little better. He had no parents and was living with his grandmother. I went to visit his grandmother. She thought for sure I was coming to let her know about all the confusion he created. I didn't say anything about that. I simply asked her if she and Marcus would like to go out to breakfast the next morning. She agreed. I brought Paul with me, and we picked them up.

There was a strong smell of marijuana in their house. We're not to judge first but show love, so we treated them to a great breakfast. I know Marcus was wondering why we were blessing them when he had stolen a bike and caused so much trouble.

We went to Walmart with them, and I'm sure they couldn't figure out what was going on. We went to the bike aisle and told Marcus that we wanted to buy him a bike, a helmet, and a lock just for him. We said, the next time you need something, you don't have to steal it, you simply ask Jesus. He will meet all your needs.

He started crying. His grandmother was crying. Paul and I were crying. I spoke up right there in the bike department and asked them if they wanted to receive Jesus today. They both said yes! I prayed with them, and they received Christ.

We got them home with a new bike, helmet, and chain lock. They hugged me so hard my neck hurt for two days, but it was worth it! I heard from Dorothy about a month later, and she told me she stopped smoking marijuana, and Marcus was doing better. She was looking for a job, and they started going to church every Sunday.

Their lives radically changed. We could have handled this in a different way, but when Jesus lives inside your heart, you still hate sin, but you love the sinner.

CHAPTER 37

YOUNG GIRLS AND BABIES

Once within two months apart, we had two teenage girls who came in and wanted to talk to me. There was nothing new about that, it happened quite frequently.

The first young woman was pregnant. She was scared and wasn't ready to have a child. She told me she remembered me talking one time in the youth group about how we are so special, and that God has made everyone for a purpose.

She was living with her mother, and the mother said she needed to get an abortion. I met with her mom. After our talk, she agreed that the baby her daughter was carrying was made by God, and an abortion would be something that they would regret.

As a ministry, we were able to make connections and get the family baby clothes, stroller, crib, and many other items to get them started.

Lisa had her baby, and all went well. Her mother had two other children. They all got saved and started going to church. I ran into Lisa sometime later. She was so happy to be a mom. She was engaged to be married and thanked me for speaking the truth in love.

CHAPTER 38

MESSAGE OF HOPE

As we travel the journey of life, there are so many people needing to know that Jesus loves them. As Christians, we are to be the light and the salt of the world. We bring light into dark situations, and we help life to become more flavorful.

We should see ourselves as carriers of hope wherever we go. Many people are looking for the truth. We are all messengers of the good news of the gospel. How exciting to look back on your life and be able to say, "Look and see what the Lord has done."

The other young woman also thought about abortion. One of my helpers and I prayed with her, and she decided she would let the baby live. After the baby was born, she gave the baby up for adoption. As a team, we were able to help many who came to find the help they needed.

We drove many to Teen Challenge in Muskegon, some to Saginaw, and others to the Teen Challenge center we had in our city. Over time, I officiated at funerals and did visitations with the sick in the hospital. Receiving clergy clearance allowed me to go into jails and prisons too. Many got saved and lives were changed. All to the glory of our Lord Jesus Christ.

CHAPTER 39

HELP IN TIME OF TROUBLE

I have written this book to help those who believe there is no hope and feel utterly helpless and full of anxiety because of past traumatic events in your life. I want you to know that there is always hope for you through Jesus Christ. Things have a way of getting better when we trust God. Jesus reminds us that all things work together for the good to those who love God and are called according to His purpose for them.

He will receive all the glory and praise. When we share our testimonies, we know we are standing by His grace and mercy. We all have a story to tell. The details of our stories may be very different, but the solution is always the same—Jesus—who is the same yesterday, today, and forever. Amen. He is the answer to healing broken lives, restoring our lives. and making us new people. If He did that for me, I am certain He will do it for you.

For me, having a family was the greatest gift from God I could ask for. When I was twenty-one-years old, I had a cyst on my right ovary. After the surgery, the doctor told me I might not ever be able to have children. At the time,

I never pictured myself living past twenty-five years of age. The way I grew up, losing both my parents at a young age, and then growing up in a place where I should have been protected and cared for instead of being beaten, slapped, disrespected, humiliated, and put down with such hard words and mean rejection, I felt like a hollow shell, not a real person.

I still strained to try and remember anyone who cared at the children's home. I could never see myself married or having children after being rejected so much as a child. I never had an example of a normal family. I could not see having a happy family ever happening for me. Even so, the possibility of never being able to have a child still bothered me. But God had other plans. It was like Him saying, "Diane, you didn't have a family growing up, so I'm going to give you an awesome family."

When I married Paul, I was amazed that someone loved me, let alone wanted to commit his life to me. Fast forward to today, and we've been married 48 years!

We were married only a few months, and I became pregnant. I was shocked, happy, and thrilled. I was still very childlike in many ways because of how I grew up. So I kept saying, "Wow! I get to have a baby."

I was so proud that I would be a mom, and I cried hard when I got the news. I prayed for a whole hour, just thanking my God that He saw fit to let me become a mother. I had never seen myself in the role of a mother.

My pregnancy went well. I read many books on what to expect at the various stages, etcetera. The older ladies at my church were very helpful and encouraging, almost like mother figures. That was nice for me, since I didn't have a mother to talk to.

Our first child finally arrived. She was beautiful. We named her Samara. I held her in my arms and cried. I remembered telling her that I would always love her and take good care of her. It was at that moment, when I held my precious little girl, all the negative emotions, physical and mental trauma and emotional abuse suddenly disappeared! God truly healed my broken heart by allowing me to have a child.

I was able to nurse her and didn't even mind getting up at night to care for her. She was a very happy baby, always smiling. The lady at the grocery store nicknamed her Smiley.

Some people have asked me over the years how I became such a great parent. I laugh and say I just know how to love. I also know what *not* to do as a parent.

With my experience of being abused and taking many years to heal, I realize, more than ever, that life and death are in the power of the tongue. What we speak over a child makes a world of difference in their self-esteem and confidence as a person.

I spoke the word of life over my children. I still do it to this very day, giving words of affirmation. I point out all their good points, gifts, and talents. I remind them that they can do all things through Christ who strengthens them. It took me many years to peel off the word curses spoken over me. We must walk in unconditional love and believe the best about others.

Our next child was born about 22 months later. I went into the hospital, and I was only there three hours when our handsome little baby boy, Hezron, was born. He didn't give me any trouble with labor or delivery. Everything went so fast! His personality is, and has been, that way all his life, a peaceful personality. As Samara got older, she did ballet and cheerleading. She was good at sports and went to community college to become a nursing assistant. Hezron loves animals, hunting, and fishing. He also played hockey from the age of five and into his 20s. He now works at Sparrow Hospital.

It was about two-and-a-half years after his birth that our beautiful daughter, Eliza, was born. God was truly blessing us with children. I love caring for them, cooking, and keeping the house clean. I love being a wife and mother.

We took our children to church, and as a family, we all learned so much from God's Word on how to operate and function as a Christian home. The Word says to train up your children in the way they should go, so when they were older they won't depart from it.

I never had a problem disciplining them the way the word teaches. I never allowed myself to be angry. I just discipline them in love. I thank God I was very careful to never repeat my past. I think that's why I was so patient, loving, kind, caring ... but still firm, because I never wanted them to have a wounded spirit. After all, a wounded spirit can be hard to heal.

Eliza was very active and happy. She was good at basketball and soccer, and even ran marathons. Eliza was very friendly. She kept her room clean, loves baking and cooking. She now has two businesses: One is cleaning, and the other business is baking. She has gone on missions trip to other countries. She brings joy everywhere she goes. She, like Samara and Hezron, love Jesus. Each of them is well liked by others in their sphere of influence.

Our fourth child, Joseph, was born three years after Eliza. He was a big boy, weighing close to ten pounds at birth, and was very long. He grew to be very tall, dark. and handsome. He was also so friendly, even as a little boy.

Joseph, much like his other siblings, was good at sports. There was a time when he was on a softball team, and every time he got to bat, he made a home run. He excelled in basketball, and just like his brother, playing hockey. When he was very young, he got little jobs mowing lawns and washing cars. Today he is a very successful real estate agent in two states. My husband and I enjoyed keeping up with all the children's schedules, homework, church, and so forth. They kept us very busy, but we still truly enjoyed being a very close family.

After our fourth child was born, my husband asked if I could get the operation a woman gets so we wouldn't have any more children. We had two boys and two girls, and he was the one working so hard to provide for us all, so I agreed.

When I went to get the surgery, the doctor told me that the operation was permanent, and I would never be able to have children again. He asked me if I was sure that we didn't want any more children. I told him, yes, I understood. So I signed a paper and was wheeled off to surgery. On the way, I prayed and asked the Lord to please let His will be done, not Paul's, not mine. Let *His* will be done. I didn't feel like I had a peace about it yet, but I simply trusted God.

Everything went great. When I got home, I stayed busy with all the family responsibilities. My husband saw a commercial about diapers. He said he guessed we wouldn't be needing those ever again. We just laughed. About a year later, I woke up feeling like I had the flu. This went on for three days. I knew I couldn't be pregnant, but I had a feeling that felt like morning sickness. I decided to get a pregnancy test done anyway. Sure enough, I was pregnant with our fifth child. This was a miracle! My doctor called it a medical miracle.

Beautiful Kathryn was born. My pregnancy with our fifth child was very special, because I knew God wanted her in this world. In the natural, it would have been impossible.

I felt honored and blessed to carry another child. This was God's will, not ours. Sometimes we make decisions in life that we think are the right ones, but thank God, He loves us so much that He allows His will to be done, not ours.

The whole pregnancy and delivery went very well, with no problems whatsoever. Kathryn was such a beautiful baby. The other children were happy when she was born. Samara was ten-years-old and my great helper. She played with Kathryn a lot and even helped change diapers when I was busy with the other children.

Katie was a very happy little girl who loved playing with dolls. When she got older she took dance lessons, was on the track team at high school, and went on to college to become a nursing assistant. She became a very good worker with the elderly that have dementia or Alzheimer's and remains working with them today.

I worked at an assisted living center as a chaplain while Katie was working there. Each day when I arrived at the center, the first thing residents would ask me is whether Katie was working that day, and what time she would be there. They all loved her, she was very kind to everyone. Even to this day, she brings so much joy and love everywhere she goes. She can see the needs of others.

Time has a way of marching on. Now all our children are grown adults, and we currently have ten grandchildren. God has been very good to us! We remain close and get together often.

A LAST THOUGHT FOR YOU

I have been told that people remember the last thing you say to them. So once again, the purpose for this book is to bring hope to anyone feeling hopeless. God can truly heal our broken hearts and restore back to us anything that has been lost.

Not only can God heal us, but He can use us in incredible ways when we allow Him to heal and restore us. Because of the various traumas or hurts we've been through, we tend to have a keen eye for those who have been hurt or rejected.

We can show them God's love and boldly share our story—our testimony. The same God that helped me can help you. God loves us all. He created you, and you are fearfully and wonderfully made. He created you and knew you when you were still in your mother's womb.

It is important that today you ask Jesus to come into your life. He will forgive you, heal you, restore you, and make you a new person.

My hope and prayer for anyone reading this book is you would gain a deep understanding that your life matters to God. This is just my story. But we all have a testimony. Remember, you didn't go through all you have gone through for no reason. I need you to know that sometimes God Himself allows things to happen so as we overcome, and by hearing our testimony, others can receive hope that they, too, can have a new life in Christ.

Never give up. Your victory might be just around the corner. Someone is waiting on the other side of your obedience to get through what you've dealt with, so they can be assured and comforted that with God all things are possible.

SCRIPTURES TO READ WHEN FEELING ALONE AND SCARED:

And we know that God causes everything to work together for the good of those who love God and are called according to his purpose for them—Romans 8:28

Father to the fatherless, defender of widows—this is God, whose dwelling is holy.—Psalm 68:5

The Lord is a shelter for the oppressed, a refuge in time of trouble. Those who know your name trust in you, for you, O Lord, do not abandon those who search for you.—Psalm 9:9-10

Anyone who belongs to Christ has become a new person. The old life is gone; a new life has begun!—2 Corinthians 5:17

Trust in the Lord with all your heart; do not depend on your own understanding. Seek his will in all you do, and he will show you which path to take.—Proverbs 3:5-6

Jesus looked at them intently and said, "Humanly speaking, it is impossible. But with God everything is possible.—Matthew 19:26

If God is for us, who can ever be against us?—Romans 8:31

For I can do everything through Christ, who gives me strength.—Philippians 4:13

Since turning my life over to Jesus Christ, these have been my favorite Bible verses. They help me remember God loves me and will help me through every tough time I face. Even now, I go through these verses to stay "fixed" and focused on what God will continue to do in my life.

If He restored me, He will do the same for you.

ABOUT THE AUTHOR

Diane Dalton went from a loving home with two parents into an orphanage at the age of seven. Her father died on the day of her mother's funeral, with no relatives willing to adopt her, her brother, and two sisters.

She lived an incredible life, surviving a very abusive childhood during her years in an orphanage. Today she has overcome all those hurts and rejection.

After ministry school, she became a youth pastor, helping many young people in the Lansing community. She also helped many who found themselves homeless and on drugs. Appointed as Woman of the Year by the *Greater Lansing Woman Magazine*, Diane is noted for her many accomplishments and ministries.

Diane is a true champion, and her story is an example for us all. Contact her at pdventures07@yahoo.com

DIANE AND TWO PASTORS PRESENTING HER A PLAQUE
FOR HER WORK WITH THE INNER-CITY TEENS

DIANE'S BEAUTIFUL FAMILY—A TRUE BLESSING FROM GOD

SAMARA AS MISS AMERICA PRE-TEEN MICHIGAN FINALIST

HEZRON AND HIS SISTER, KATHRYN

BROKEN BUT FIXED

Eliza and her family

Joseph and his family

DIANE DALTON

KATHRYN (KATIE) AND HER HUSBAND

JOSEPH AND KURSTIN'S WEDDING IN 2008
AT SANIBEL ISLAND

Dear Mom,   1-29-02

Happy Birthday! We wanted to write you a little note to let
you know how much you mean to all us kids. First of all we
are all so proud of what you've done with us. Teaching us
about the Lord has shown true love. Not just giving us
everything we want, but investing more Spiritual things in
our lives, shows how much you really care. You have been a
perfect example of how we are to live as we are all reaching
adulthood. Being a servant without much recognition, and
staying in such close touch with the Lord has been an
amazing example that we will never forget. We all have
different memories of our childhood with you, but some
memories we all share. When you would pack our lunch
and write an encouraging note on our napkin. When you
would, and still do, pray for us every night before bed.
When we would go to Caesar land and run around until we
nearly pass out. When you would take each of us on an
"outing." When we would run around the living room with
pots and pans, banging them to "The Lord's army." There
are so many other great memories that we all cherish.
Again, we want to say that we are so proud of how much
time, effort and prayer you have invested in us. It will
definitely pay off, when we know how to train our kids in
the way of the Lord as you have trained us. Thanks for
being such an incredible mother. We love you.
                         Sincerely,
                         Your Children